Children'
Activity Book & Journal
My Trip to Hawaii

TravelJournalBooks

CONTENTS

Hi, I hope you enjoy this book. It is jam packed with cool stuff for you to do from crosswords, word searches, drawing, coloring and quizzes. It has loads of fun things for you to do in Hawaii.

Have FUN in HAWAII

FOR YOUR PARENTS

We hope you enjoy your trip and thank you for buying our book, keep it safe as it is a great keepsake of your child's early years.

If you like this book, please leave us a review or provide feedback.

We have books for a number of holiday destinations at:

www.TravelJournalBooks.com

Bonus:
We have provided a bonus for you on page 83. We hope it helps.

This is my Journal

My Name:

Age:

Parent's name:

Tel:

Address:

Important Information

Cool Places in Hawaii for Kids

Hawaii Volcanoes National Park	✓
Puuhonua o Honaunau National Historical Park	
Kahalu'u Beach Park	
Atlantis Submarine	
Maui Ocean Center	
Bishop Museum	
Polynesian Cultural Center	
Hawaiian Kids Discovery Center	
Kauai Backcountry Adventures	
Na 'Āina Kai Botanical Gardens	
Kalaupapa Guided Mule Ride	
Big Wind Kite Factory	

Hulopoe Beach	
Mokupapapa Discovery Center	
Maui Golf and Sports Park	
Hawaiian Waters Adventure Park	
Wet n Wild Hawaii	
Dolphin Quest	
BOB's Hawaii Adventure	
Kahoma Ranch	
Kihei Aquatic Center	
Sea Life Park	
Honolulu Zoo	
Waikiki Aquarium	
Pana'ewa Rainforest Zoo and Gardens	

Do your own research to find out what other places you would like to visit

Best Websites to Research Further

Do some more research on the internet and add other cool places you find:

www.TravelJournalBooks.com/Hawaii We keep this fully updated with the best places
www.wikipedia.org/wiki/hawaii
www.gohawaii.com
www.lonelyplanet.com/usa/hawaii
www.travelsmarthawaii.com
www.Hawaii.com
www.101thingstodo.com/

More cool places I want to visit on our trip

1. _____

2. _____

3. _____

4. _____

5. _____

6. _____

7. _____

8. _____

9. _____

10. _____

11. _____

12. _____

13. _____

14. _____

15. _____

Who do I want to send postcards to?

Name:
Address:

Name:
Address:

Name:
Address:

Name:
Address:

Name:

Address:

Name:

Address:

Name:

Address:

Name:

Address:

Name:

Address:

Packing List

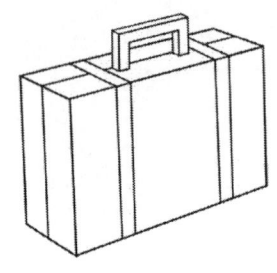

✓	This Book
	Tickets
	Passport
	Money
	Chargers
	Batteries
	Book to read
	Camera
	Tablet
	Sun glasses
	Sun cream
	Medication
	Jacket

	Toys
	Games
	Watch
	Snacks
	Umbrella
	Towel
	Guide book
	Add more below ...

Activities to do on the way to Hawaii

Cool facts, word search, crossword and other fun activities

Answers and solutions are at the back of the book

Cool Facts About Hawaii for Kids

- The word Hawaii is from the Proto-Polynesian "hawaiki", meaning 'place of the gods' or 'homeland'

- Hawaii state's nickname is "Aloha State'

- 'Aloha' is one of the most used words in Hawaiian Language. Aloha can be used both as 'hello' and 'goodbye'

- Mount Waialeale on Kauai is one of the wettest place on earth. It receives annually 460 inches of rain

- Mauna Loa, the world's biggest volcano, presents out-of-the-world experience on Earth. NASA Astronauts got trained for moon voyages by walking on its lava fields

- Haleakalā (means 'House of the Sun') is the world's largest dormant volcano

- The Hawaiian alphabet has only 12 letters: a, e, h, i, k, l, m, n, o, p, u, w

- The Happy Face Spider is only found on the islands of Oahu, Molokai, Maui, and Hawaii

- The State of Hawaii is comprised of 132 islands, eight major islands (Hawaii, Maui, Kahoolawe, Moloka, Lanai, Oahu, Kauai, and Niiahu) and 124 islets, reefs, and shoals

- Hawaii is the only US state with a tropical rain forest

- The Big Island (Hawaii Island) is getting bigger by about 42 acres each year because of the continuous eruption of the Kīlauea Volcano. It's been erupting for 30 years.

- Kauai, also known as the 'Garden Isle' is famous for its jagged green mountains, white-sand beaches and tropical landscapes. More than 60 Hollywood movies have been filmed here, including Jurassic Park

Big Hawaii Word Search

Hawaii

Pearl Harbor

Kauai

Haleakalā

Ka Lae

Honolulu

Aloha

Mauna Loa

Hawaiki

Iolani Palace

A	O	W	E	U	Q	T	K	R	P	E	A	L	A	K	H
W	L	L	J	O	Z	N	N	D	J	L	A	W	A	W	A
H	A	O	Y	N	N	K	R	B	C	T	K	R	T	A	W
H	S	S	H	M	I	T	E	L	I	L	I	I	I	K	A
U	U	S	H	A	K	N	W	O	T	A	G	R	O	E	I
Z	B	E	U	U	D	C	N	H	U	V	X	I	L	N	I
I	M	A	L	N	N	A	T	A	O	N	S	T	A	G	E
T	U	S	U	A	L	G	K	L	I	F	J	M	N	S	E
Q	L	X	L	L	P	M	T	E	E	J	K	D	I	B	X
I	O	X	O	O	U	T	Y	A	Z	S	D	G	P	X	N
K	C	O	N	A	P	I	J	K	N	N	O	P	A	I	K
I	W	Y	O	O	G	P	M	A	O	D	O	F	L	P	W
A	K	W	H	P	U	Z	X	L	P	R	C	T	A	A	L
W	E	D	G	B	U	S	S	A	I	O	V	R	C	E	G
A	H	L	L	G	K	J	E	Q	O	P	N	B	E	E	V
H	V	P	E	A	R	L	H	A	R	B	O	R	C	I	R

Great Hawaii Crossword

Across

2. Seventh largest of the Hawaiian Islands
4. Largest volcano on Earth
5. One of the most used words in Hawaiian Language

Down

1. Hawaiian dance
3. Capital of Hawaii

Link Up Hawaii

Link the letters, to make a word or phrase

Iolani	Harbor
Aloha	Falls
Ka	State
Big	Island
Pearl	Kea
Bishop	Palace
Kahiwa	Isle
Mauna	Lae
Garden	Loa
Mauna	Museum

Code Puzzle

Use the number codes to find the words (Tip 1=A, 2=B, 3=C)

8	15	14	15	12	21	12	21

11	1		12	1	5
		▓			

13	20		23	1	9	1	12	5	1	12	5
		▓									

8	1	23	1	9	9

23	1	9	12	21	11	21		18	9	22	5	18
							▓					

9	15	12	1	14	9		16	1	12	1	3	5
						▓						

Tile Puzzle

Rearrange the tiles to reveal the answer

Clue: Largest volcano on Earth

| A | L | UN | OA | MA |

_____

Clue: One of the wettest place on earth

| NT | MOU | ALE | WAI | ALE |

_____

Clue: Attacked by the Japanese on December 7, 1941

| RL | BOR | PEA | HAR |

_____

Clue: Hawaii's longest waterfall

| IWA | KAH | LS | FAL |

_____

Mix Up

Unscramble each of the anagram clue words.

Copy the letters in the numbered cells to other cells with the same number to reveal the hidden message.

HAOLA   (Example)

A	L	O	H	A

IIHNAU

	I		H		U

3

SSURJAIC RAPK

	U		A		S		C			A		K

   8   4

NGAERD SLIE

	A		D		N			S		E

   11

IIAAHW

	A		A		I

6

IGB IDSNAL

	I		▓		S		A		D

9   5

SPBHIO MMUUES

B		S		O		▓	M		S		U	

1   2

AMNAU OLA

M		U		A	▓	L		A

7   10

Hidden Message

1   2   3   4   5   6   7   8   9   10   11

The Fallen Message Puzzle

Each letter appears in the correct column, but below where it should be.
You must put the letters back in the grid to rebuild the message.

▓	W		L		O		E		▓
T		▓		A		A			I
▓	▓		N		O			▓	▓
	O	U		▓		R	I		

			H		W	A		
	O	E	L	J	O	R	I	
T	O	U	N	A	T	M	I	I
Y	W	E	R	C	O	Y	E	P

25

Code Cracker

1. Solve the numbers puzzle

2. Convert the answer to a letter (1=A, 2=B, 3=C).
   Crack the secret code word.

				1. Number		2. Letter
11	-	10	=		=	
18	-	6	=		=	
22	-	7	=		=	
20	-	12	=		=	
1	+	0	=		=	
22	-	3	=		=	
5	+	15	=		=	
15	-	14	=		=	
9	+	11	=		=	
7	-	2	=		=	

Number Chains

1. Work out the math puzzle for each column below
2. Find the secret word, using the code (1=A, 2=B, 3=C)

6	11	16	5	16	20	18	9
+	+	+	+	-	+	-	+
3	3	3	14	12	8	6	7
=	=	=	=	=	=	=	=
+	-	+	-	+	-	+	-
11	13	11	14	5	10	13	8
=	=	=	=	=	=	=	=
-	+	-	+	+	+	-	+
12	14	16	10	3	3	13	13
=	=	=	=	=	=	=	=

Enter the letters above using the number code (1=A, 2=B, 3=C)

A-Mazing Maze

Can you find your way through the maze?

Color Hawaii

Color the USA Flag

Colors: Red, white and blue

Hawaii Trip Diary

Write a daily diary during your trip.

Day 1   Tip! Parents see page 83

Date: _____

Weather: _____

What we did today

_____

_____

_____

_____

_____

_____

_____

Cool food of the day: _____

What I liked best today: _____

Funny thing of the day: _____

Draw something you saw today

My picture is of: _____

Day 2

Date: _____

Weather: _____

What we did today

_____

_____

_____

_____

_____

_____

_____

_____

Cool food of the day: _____

What I liked best today: _____

Funny thing of the day: _____

Draw something you saw today

My picture is of: _____

Day 3

Date: _____

Weather: _____

What we did today

_____

_____

_____

_____

_____

_____

_____

Cool food of the day: _____

What I liked best today: _____

Funny thing of the day: _____

Draw something you saw today

My picture is of: _____

Day 4

Date: _____

Weather: _____

What we did today

_____

_____

_____

_____

_____

_____

_____

Cool food of the day: _____

What I liked best today: _____

Funny thing of the day: _____

Draw something you saw today

My picture is of: _____

Day 5   Tip! Send your postcards

Date: _____

Weather: _____

What we did today

_____

_____

_____

_____

_____

_____

_____

_____

Cool food of the day: _____

What I liked best today: _____

Funny thing of the day: _____

Draw something you saw today

My picture is of: _____

Day 6

Date: _____

Weather: _____

What we did today

_____

_____

_____

_____

_____

_____

_____

Cool food of the day: _____

What I liked best today: _____

Funny thing of the day: _____

Draw something you saw today

My picture is of: _____

Day 7

Date: _____

Weather: _____

What we did today

_____

_____

_____

_____

_____

_____

_____

Cool food of the day: _____

What I liked best today: _____

Funny thing of the day: _____

Draw something you saw today

My picture is of: _____

Day 8

Date: _____

Weather: _____

What we did today

_____

_____

_____

_____

_____

_____

_____

Cool food of the day: _____

What I liked best today: _____

Funny thing of the day: _____

Draw something you saw today

My picture is of: _____

Day 9

Date: _____

Weather: _____

What we did today

_____

_____

_____

_____

_____

_____

_____

Cool food of the day: _____

What I liked best today: _____

Funny thing of the day: _____

Draw something you saw today

My picture is of: _____

Day 10

Date: _____

Weather: _____

What we did today

_____

_____

_____

_____

_____

_____

Cool food of the day: _____

What I liked best today: _____

Funny thing of the day: _____

Draw something you saw today

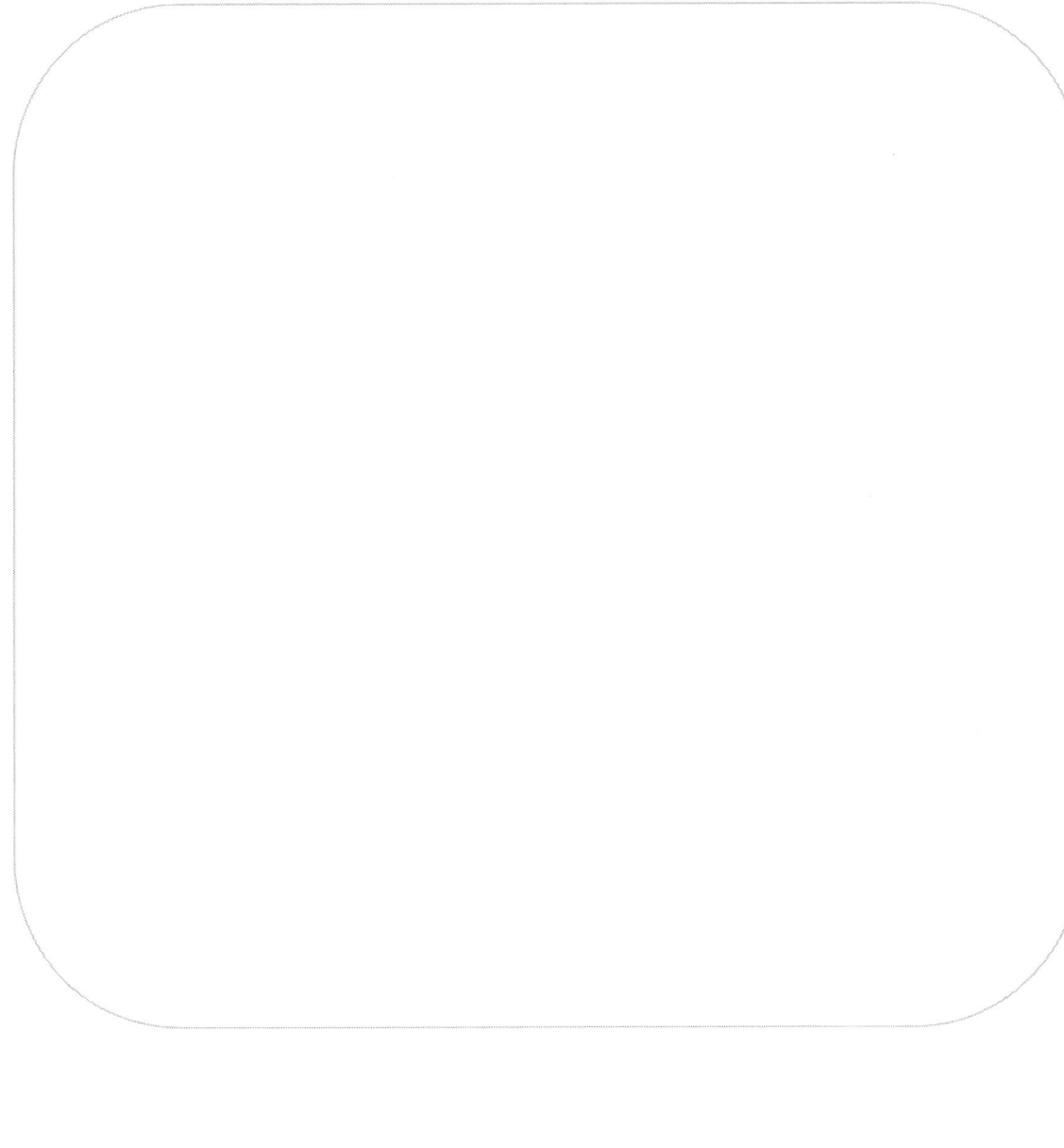

My picture is of: _____

Day 11

Date: _____

Weather: _____

What we did today

_____

_____

_____

_____

_____

_____

_____

Cool food of the day: _____

What I liked best today: _____

Funny thing of the day: _____

Draw something you saw today

My picture is of: _____

Day 12

Date:

Weather:

What we did today

_____

_____

_____

_____

_____

_____

_____

Cool food of the day:

What I liked best today:

Funny thing of the day:

Draw something you saw today

My picture is of: _____

Day 13

Date: _____

Weather: _____

What we did today

_____

_____

_____

_____

_____

_____

_____

Cool food of the day: _____

What I liked best today: _____

Funny thing of the day: _____

Draw something you saw today

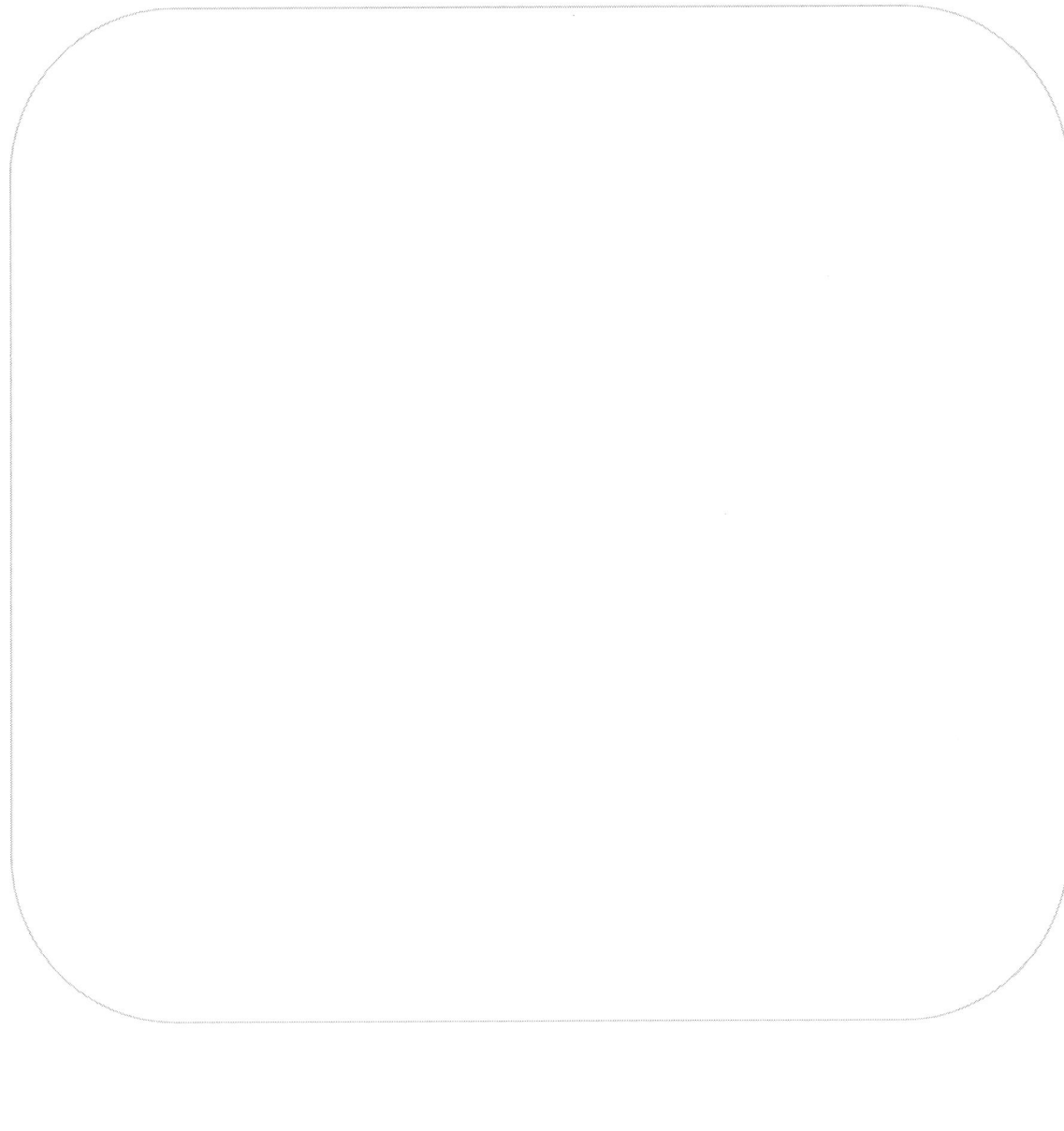

My picture is of: _____

Day 14

Date: _____

Weather: _____

What we did today

_____

_____

_____

_____

_____

_____

_____

Cool food of the day: _____

What I liked best today: _____

Funny thing of the day: _____

Draw something you saw today

My picture is of: _____

Activities for the Trip Home

Quiz, drawing and coloring fun, for your trip home

Answers and solutions are at the back of the book

Big Quiz

(Circle the correct answer)

1. What is the capital city of Hawaii?

   Honolulu   Kalawao

   Kauai   Maui

2. What is the largest volcano on Earth?

   Mauna Loa   Mount Waialeale

   Ka Lae   Niihau

3. One of the wettest places on earth

   Mauna Loa   Mount Waialeale

   Ka Lae   Niihau

4. The only royal palace in the USA

   Iolani Palace   Pearl Harbor

   Big Island   Lei

5. How many letters does the Hawaiian alphabet have?

   13 letters   12 letters

   17 letters   15 letters

6. What is the state nickname of Hawaii?

   Maui   Ka Lae

   Honolulu   Aloha State

7. Park that is home to two active volcanoes, Kilauea and Mauna Loa

   Hawaii Volcanoes National Park   Kahalu'u Beach Park

   Polynesian Cultural Center   Maui Ocean Center

8. What is the seventh largest of the Hawaiian Islands?

   Niihau   Lanai

   Molokai   Oahu

9. What is the world's largest dormant volcano?

   Kauai   Aloha

   Haleakalā   Iolani Palace

10. A United States Navy deep-water naval base which was attacked by the
    Japanese on December 7, 1941

    Iolani Palace   Pearl Harbor

    Molokai   Honolulu

11. What is Hawaii's longest waterfall?

    Niihau   Kahoolawe
    Kauai   Kahiwa Falls

12. What is the oldest of the Hawaiian Islands?

    Maui   Honolulu
    Kauai   Oahu

13. Kauai is also known as

    Garden Isle   Entertainment
    Aloha State   National Archive

14. What is the largest museum in the state of Hawaii?

    Bishop Museum   Hawaiian Kids Discovery Center
    Polynesian Cultural Center   Maui Ocean Center

15. A wreath of any of nature's gifts (flowers, leaves seeds, nuts etc.)
    presented upon arriving or leaving as a symbol of affection

    Lei   Molokai
    Iuau   Kauai

Draw Hawaii

Draw some of the cool things you saw in Hawaii, during your trip

Color the USA Flag

Colors: Red, White and Blue

Things I will remember from our trip

Favorite Places we visited on our Trip

We hope you enjoyed your trip to Hawaii!

Don't forget to thank Mom and Dad

Useful Resources for Mom & Dad

Children's Shoe Sizes

UK	EUROPE	US	Japan
4	20	4½ or 5	12 ½
4 ½	21	5 or 5½	13
5	21 or 22	5½ or 6	13 ½
5 ½	22	6	13½ or 14
6	23	6½ or 7	14 or 14½
6 ½	23 or 24	7 ½	14½ or 15
7	24	7½ or 8	15
7 ½	25	8 or 9	15 ½
8	25 or 26	8½ or 9	16
8 ½	26	9½	16 ½
9	27	9½ or 10	16 ½ or 17
10	28	10½ or 11	17 ½
10½ or 11	29	11½ or 12	18
11 ½	30	12½	18 or 18 ½
12	31	13	19 or 19 ½
12 ½	31	13 or 13½	19 ½ or 20
13	32	1	20
13 ½	32 ½	1 ½	20 ½
1	33	1½ or 2	21
2	34	2½ or 3	22

Children's Clothing Sizes

UK	EUROPE	US	Australia
12m	80cm	12-18m	12m
18m	80-86cm	18-24m	18m
24m	86-92cm	23-24m	2
2-3	92-98cm	2T	3
3-4	98-104cm	4T	4
3-5	104-110cm	5	5
5-6	110-116cm	6	6
6-7	116-122cm	6X-7	7
7-8	122-128cm	7 to 8	8
8-9	128-134cm	9 to 10	9
9-10	134-140cm	10	10
10-11	140-146cm	11	11
11-12	146-152cm	14	12

Women's Shoe Sizes

UK	EUROPE	US	Japan
3	35 ½	5	22 ½
3 ½	36	5 ½	23
4	37	6	23
4 ½	37 ½	6 ½	23 ½
5	38	7	24
5 ½	39	7 ½	24
6	39 ½	8	24 ½
6 ½	40	8 ½	25
7	41	9 ½	25 ½
7 ½	41 ½	10	26
8	42	10 ½	26 ½

Women's Clothes Sizes

UK	US	Japan	France / Spain	Germany	Italy	Australia
6/8	6	7-9	36	34	40	8
10	8	9-11	38	36	42	10
12	10	11-13	40	38	44	12
14	12	13-15	42	39	46	14
16	14	15-17	44	40	48	16
18	16	17-19	46	42	50	18
20	18	19-21	48	44	52	20

Men's Shoe Sizes

UK	EUROPE	US	Japan
6	38 ½	6 ½	24 ½
6 ½	39	7	25
7	40	7 ½	25 ½
7 ½	41	8	26
8	42	8 ½	27 ½
8 ½	43	9	27 ½
9	43 ½	9 ½	28
9 ½	44	10	28 ½
10	44	10 ½	28 ½
10 ½	44 ½	11	29
11	45	12	29 ½

Men's Suit / Coat / Sweater Sizes

UK / US / Aus	EU / Japan	General
32	42	Small
34	44	Small
36	46	Small
38	48	Medium
40	50	Large
42	52	Large
44	54	Extra Large
46	56	Extra Large

Men's Pants / Trouser Sizes (Waist)

UK / US	Europe
32	81 cm
34	86 cm
36	91 cm
38	97 cm
40	102 cm
42	107 cm

Puzzles Answers and Solutions

Big Hawaii Word Search

Hawaii   Honolulu

Pearl Harbor   Aloha

Kauai   Mauna Loa

Haleakalā   Hawaiki

Ka Lae   Iolani Palace

A	O	W	E	U	Q	T	K	R	P	E	A	L	A	K	H
W	L	L	J	O	Z	N	N	D	J	L	A	W	A	W	A
H	A	O	Y	N	N	K	R	B	C	T	K	R	T	A	W
H	S	S	H	M	I	T	E	L	I	L	I	I	I	K	A
U	U	S	H	A	K	N	W	O	T	A	G	R	O	E	I
Z	B	E	U	U	D	C	N	H	U	V	X	I	L	N	I
I	M	A	L	N	N	A	T	A	O	N	S	T	A	G	E
T	U	S	U	A	L	G	K	L	I	F	J	M	N	S	E
Q	L	X	L	L	P	M	T	E	E	J	K	D	I	B	X
I	O	X	O	O	U	T	Y	A	Z	S	D	G	P	X	N
K	C	O	N	A	P	I	J	K	N	N	O	P	A	I	K
I	W	Y	O	O	G	P	M	A	O	D	O	F	L	P	W
A	K	W	H	P	U	Z	X	L	P	R	C	T	A	A	L
W	E	D	G	B	U	S	S	A	I	O	V	R	C	E	G
A	H	L	L	G	K	J	E	Q	O	P	N	B	E	E	V
H	V	P	E	A	R	L	H	A	R	B	O	R	C	I	R

Great Hawaii Crossword

```
                              ┌───┐
                              │¹  │
                              │ H │
      ┌───┬───┬───┬───┬───┼───┤
      │²  │   │   │³  │   │ U │
      │ N │ I │ I │ H │ A │   │
      └───┴───┴───┼───┼───┼───┤
                  │ O │   │ L │
                  ├───┤   ├───┤
                  │ N │   │ A │
                  ├───┤   └───┘
                  │ O │
┌───┬───┬───┬───┬───┼───┼───┬───┐
│⁴  │   │   │   │   │   │   │   │
│ M │ A │ U │ N │ A │ L │ O │ A │
└───┴───┴───┴───┴───┼───┼───┴───┘
                    │ U │
              ┌───┬───┼───┼───┬───┐
              │⁵  │   │   │   │   │
              │ A │ L │ O │ H │ A │
              └───┴───┼───┼───┴───┘
                      │ U │
                      └───┘
```

Across

2. Seventh largest of the Hawaiian Islands
4. Largest volcano on Earth
5. One of the most used words in Hawaiian Language

Down

1. Hawaiian dance
3. Capital of Hawaii

Link Up Hawaii

Link the letters, to make a word or phrase

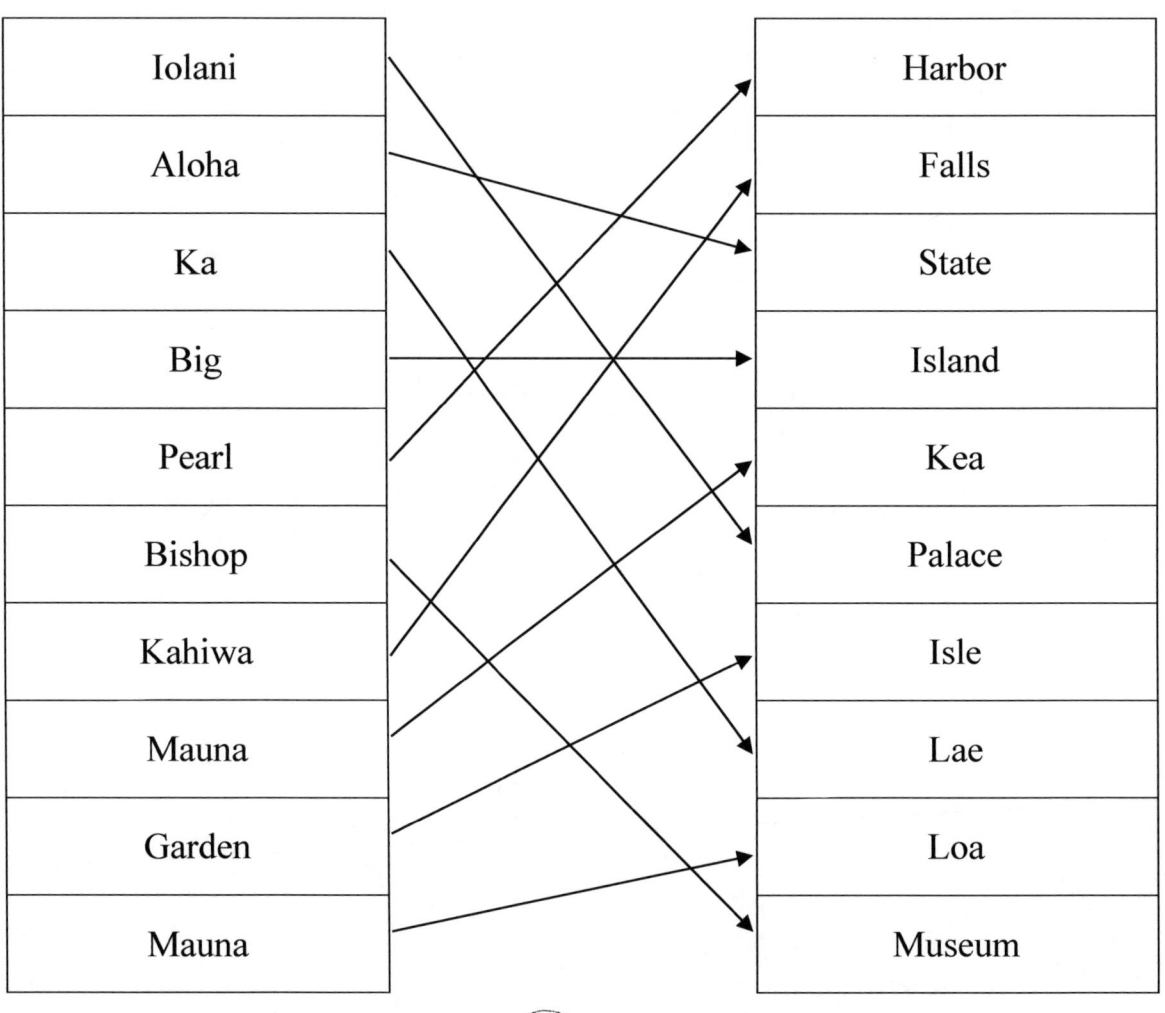

Iolani	Harbor
Aloha	Falls
Ka	State
Big	Island
Pearl	Kea
Bishop	Palace
Kahiwa	Isle
Mauna	Lae
Garden	Loa
Mauna	Museum

Code Puzzle

Use the number codes to find the words (Tip 1=A, 2=B, 3=C)

8	15	14	15	12	21	12	21
H	O	N	O	L	U	L	U

11	1		12	1	5
K	A		L	A	E

13	20		23	1	9	1	12	5	1	12	5
M	T		W	A	I	A	L	E	A	L	E

8	1	23	1	9	9
H	A	W	A	I	I

23	1	9	12	21	11	21		18	9	22	5	18
W	A	I	L	U	K	U		R	I	V	E	R

9	15	12	1	14	9		16	1	12	1	3	5
I	O	L	A	N	I		P	A	L	A	C	E

Tile Puzzle

Rearrange the tiles to reveal the answer

Clue: Largest volcano on Earth

A	L	UN	OA	MA

MAUNA LOA

Clue: One of the wettest place on earth

NT	MOU	ALE	WAI	ALE

MOUNT WAIALEALE

Clue: Attacked by the Japanese on December 7, 1941

RL	BOR	PEA	HAR

PEARL HARBOR

Clue: Hawaii's longest waterfall

IWA	KAH	LS	FAL

KAHIWA FALLS

Mix Up

Unscramble each of the anagram clue words.

Copy the letters in the numbered cells to other cells with the same number to reveal the hidden message.

HAOLA   (Example)

A	L	O	H	A

IIHNAU

N	I	I	H	A	U
			3		

SSURJAIC RAPK

J	U	R	A	S	S	I	C		P	A	R	K
	8									4		

NGAERD SLIE

G	A	R	D	E	N		I	S	L	E
	11									

IIAAHW

H	A	W	A	I	I
6					

IGB IDSNAL

B	I	G		I	S	L	A	N	D
9						5			

SPBHIO MMUUES

B	I	S	H	O	P		M	U	S	E	U	M
					1					2		

AMNAU OLA

M	A	U	N	A		L	O	A
	7						10	

Hidden Message

P	E	A	R	L	H	A	R	B	O	R
1	2	3	4	5	6	7	8	9	10	11

The Fallen Message Puzzle

Each letter appears in the correct column, but below where it should be.
You must put the letters back in the grid to rebuild the message.

	W	E	L	C	O	M	E	
T	O		H	A	W	A	I	I
		E	N	J	O	Y		
Y	O	U	R		T	R	I	P

			H		W	A	
	O	E	L	J	O	R	I
T	O	U	N	A	T	M	I	I
Y	W	E	R	C	O	Y	E	P

Code Cracker

3. Solve the numbers puzzle

4. Convert the answer to a letter (1=A, 2=B, 3=C).
   Crack the secret code word.

				2. Number			2. Letter
11	-	10	=	1	=		A
18	-	6	=	12	=		L
22	-	7	=	15	=		O
20	-	12	=	8	=		H
1	+	0	=	1	=		A
22	-	3	=	19	=		S
5	+	15	=	20	=		T
15	-	14	=	1	=		A
9	+	11	=	20	=		T
7	-	2	=	5	=		E

Number Chains

3. Work out the math puzzle for each column below
4. Find the secret word, using the code (1=A, 2=B, 3=C)

6	11	16	5	16	20	18	9
+	+	+	+	-	+	-	+
3	3	3	14	12	8	6	7
=	=	=	=	=	=	=	=
9	**14**	**19**	**19**	**4**	**28**	**12**	**16**
+	-	+	-	+	-	+	-
11	13	11	14	5	10	13	8
=	=	=	=	=	=	=	=
20	**1**	**30**	**5**	**9**	**18**	**25**	**8**
-	+	-	+	+	+	-	+
12	14	16	10	3	3	13	13
=	=	=	=	=	=	=	=
8	**15**	**14**	**15**	**12**	**21**	**12**	**21**

H	O	N	O	L	U	L	U

Enter the letters above using the number code (1=A, 2=B, 3=C)

97

Big Quiz

(Circle the correct answer)

10. What is the capital city of Hawaii?

   <u>Honolulu</u>   Kalawao

   Kauai   Maui

11. What is the largest volcano on Earth?

   <u>Mauna Loa</u>   Mount Waialeale

   Ka Lae   Niihau

12. One of the wettest places on earth

   Mauna Loa   **<u>Mount Waialeale</u>**

   Ka Lae   Niihau

13. The only royal palace in the USA

   <u>Iolani Palace</u>   Pearl Harbor

   Big Island .   Lei

14. How many letters does the Hawaiian alphabet have?

   13 letters   **<u>12 letters</u>**

   17 letters   15 letters

15. What is the state nickname of Hawaii?

Maui   Ka Lae

Honolulu   **Aloha State**

16. Park that is home to two active volcanoes, Kilauea and Mauna Loa

Hawaii Volcanoes National Park   Kahalu'u Beach Park

Polynesian Cultural Center   Maui Ocean Center

17. What is the seventh largest of the Hawaiian Islands?

Niihau   Lanai

Molokai   Oahu

18. What is the world's largest dormant volcano?

Kauai   Aloha

Haleakalā   Iolani Palace

10. A United States Navy deep-water naval base which was attacked by the Japanese on December 7, 1941

Iolani Palace   **Pearl Harbor**

Molokai   Honolulu

11. What is Hawaii's longest waterfall?

Niihau   Kahoolawe

Kauai   **Kahiwa Falls**

12. What is the oldest of the Hawaiian Islands?

Maui   Honolulu

Kauai   Oahu

13. Kauai is also known as

Garden Isle   Entertainment

Aloha State   National Archive

14. What is the largest museum in the state of Hawaii?

Bishop Museum   Hawaiian Kids Discovery Center

Polynesian Cultural Center Maui Ocean Center

15. A wreath of any of nature's gifts (flowers, leaves seeds, nuts etc.)
    presented upon arriving or leaving as a symbol of affection

Lei   Molokai

Iuau   Kauai

Made in the USA
San Bernardino, CA
15 August 2015